The Coronation Ch

and the Stone of Destiny

by James Wilkinson
New photographs by Malcolm Crowthers

Royal Church and Royal Chair

To the east of Edward the Confessor's Chapel in Westminster Abbey, raised on a dais, stands the oldest piece of furniture in Britain still used for its original purpose: the Coronation Chair. It has been used at every Coronation since at least 1399 and even, possibly, before that. Today it is but a shadow of what it once was. But while its appearance has deteriorated through age, use and abuse, its significance has been enhanced at each successive Coronation. It has long been an iconic item steeped in historical associations, older than the crown jewels and gazed at in awe by the Abbey's millions of visitors.

For a Coronation the Chair is placed in the sanctuary facing the high altar. The Sovereign sits in the Chair to be crowned and anointed. The Chair is not the same as the throne, which is placed further west and in which the Sovereign sits to receive the homage of representatives of the bishops and peers.

The Chair was originally made to house the Stone of Destiny after it was captured from the Scots by King Edward I in 1296. The Stone is the seat on which the Scottish kings had been inaugurated for hundreds of years and its capture by Edward, along with other loot, sealed his conquest of Scotland. Edward had the Chair made for the Stone and placed it in King Edward the Confessor's Chapel. But that is only part of the story. The history of the Stone, the legends and myths which have grown up around it, and the events in which the Stone and the Chair have played a central role in the 700 hundred years since it was captured, make an astonishing story. The Stone has the power to raise passions, even today. The empty compartment beneath the seat speaks eloquently of those passions. For it was in 1996 that the then Prime Minister, John Major, decided to advise Her Majesty the Queen to return the Stone to Scotland – exactly 700 years after it was taken. It was a decision which reignited strong feelings on both sides of the border. The Stone will still play its critical role at the next Coronation when it will be brought back and reinstalled in the Chair. But that very act itself will once more renew debate: is it a symbol of conquest or a tangible sign of the peaceful union of England and Scotland?

The Chair itself is a remarkable object. Throughout the ages it has survived against the odds. Initially it was little more than a trophy case, housed

OPPOSITE: *Westminster Abbey – the place of Coronation since 1066.*

LEFT: *One of the four lions supporting the Chair.*
OPPOSITE: *The Coronation Chair east of Henry V's tomb.*

in the monastery in the care of the monks. Henry IV was the first king who we know for certain from contemporary documents sat in the Chair for his Coronation. When King Henry VIII dissolved the monasteries (1536–40) and plundered their wealth, Westminster Abbey fared better than most – perhaps because it was a place for the crowning and burying of monarchs – and the Chair and Stone survived. After Charles I was beheaded and Oliver Cromwell assumed power, instead of being destroyed like the Coronation regalia as a hated symbol of monarchy, the Chair and Stone were taken to Westminster Hall for his installation as Lord Protector. It later survived the depredations of Westminster School boys who carved their names on it; the Victorians who painted it brown; and the Second World War, during which it was taken to Gloucester Cathedral for safe-keeping. Now, it is the object that visitors to the Abbey from all over the world most want to see.

But to start at the beginning…

Edward I seizes the Stone

In 1272, King Edward I succeeded his father, Henry III, the king who had rebuilt Westminster Abbey in honour of its founder King Edward the Confessor, who had died in 1065. Edward I was a powerful and energetic king. He fought to bring Scotland and Wales under his control and it was during one of his campaigns in Scotland that he captured the Stone of Destiny. The year was 1296. After a fierce battle at Dunbar, Edward defeated the forces of John Balliol, King of the Scots, who eventually surrendered. In an effort to wipe out any claims to Scottish independence, Edward's forces seized the Scottish regalia, chest-loads of records and, on a detour to Scone, the Stone itself – the great symbol of Scottish nationhood. His purpose in seizing the Stone was to make sure that in future Scotland was to have no other king but Edward and his descendants, and to show that Scotland had been truly conquered. It was a particular insult to the Scots, as the Stone had always played an important part in the inauguration of Scottish kings. (The Pope, largely under pressure from the English, had always refused permission for the Kings of Scotland to be crowned and anointed; they were 'inaugurated' instead.)

Scone lies on the east bank of the river Tay just over a mile from Perth and about 40 miles north of Edinburgh. Today the site is dominated by Scone Palace, the home of the Earls of Mansfield, but in ancient times it was an exceptionally important site, first to the Picts and later to the Scots. In 1114, Alexander I founded a monastic church on the site. In 1249 Alexander III was inaugurated here – the first such inauguration of which we know the details and the first one which describes how the Stone was used. The Stone was kept in the monastery and brought out to be placed in front of a cross on nearby Moot Hill where the ceremony took place. Traditionally, stone had been involved with inauguration ceremonies since ancient days. Both in Scotland and Ireland such ceremonies involved the king placing his feet in footsteps carved in stone. Being old and permanent, stone symbolised stability.

OPPOSITE: *The Stone of Destiny with one of its two iron rings.*

Edward's victory at Dunbar was not the end of his problems with Scotland. Two years later the Abbot of Scone still supported Scottish independence, so the English sacked the monastery, smashing the windows and doors and ripping the roof off the church, the cloisters and the dormitory. But Scottish ambitions were not to be held back. In 1314, at the Battle of Bannockburn, Scotland under Robert

Bruce reaffirmed its independence and in 1329 the Pope finally agreed that Scottish kings had a right to be crowned and anointed. So it was that, in 1331, five-year-old David II, the son of Robert Bruce, became the first Scottish king to be crowned and anointed: a ceremony which took place at Scone, despite the absence of the Stone. The church and surrounding buildings were finally destroyed in 1559. Today nothing, save a few architectural fragments, survives.

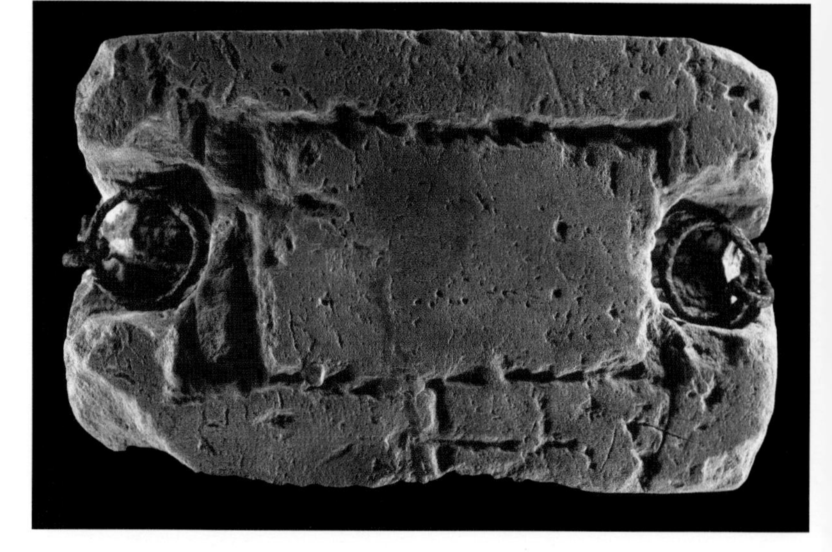

The top of the Stone has a rectangle cut in it, perhaps the start of a hollow to house a relic.

But how did the Stone of Destiny, an unimpressive lump of sandstone, acquire such a status? The myth is that the Stone was said to have been Jacob's pillow, on which he rested his head when he dreamed of angels ascending a ladder to heaven. It was said that it was taken from Egypt or Palestine first to Spain by Scota, Pharaoh's daughter, then to Ireland and finally to Scotland. The myth may date from the ninth century, when the Scots absorbed the indigenous Picts who lived in the north-east of the country. The Scots may well have claimed that the Stone they brought with them symbolised their kingship because of a prophecy that wherever the Stone was, there the Scots would reign. On the other hand the myth may simply have been invented after Edward I seized it. When he claimed lordship over the Scots by reason of having the Stone, the Scots may have countered with the legend that wherever the Stone was, the Scots would reign – with the ironic implication that they now had overlordship in England. Edward would not have been impressed by such wordplay.

Though the first reliable reference to the Stone dates from 1249, the first time it was given a specific name was probably about 1304–6 when it was called the 'Pharaoh's Stone', reflecting its mythical origin. It has rejoiced in a variety of names since then: Jacob's Pillow, the Royal Stone, the Stone of Scotland, the Coronation Stone, the Stone of Destiny (by which it is most commonly known today) and the Stone of Scone, which is perhaps the most authentic current name. This name can be traced back to 1327.

The Stone, to say the least, is dull. A simple block of sandstone roughly hewn, pockmarked and cracked, and with a metal ring at each end attached with a single link. It is not intrinsically valuable. It has undoubtedly suffered over the centuries, principally when it was broken in two during the 1950 theft from the Abbey. It is 67cms (27ins) long, 42cms (17ins) deep and 26·5cms (10·5ins) high. Cut into the surface is a rectangular groove. It is possible this was done as the first stage in making a shallow hollow in the surface, perhaps to contain some relic. Part of the rectangle is professionally cut, but the mason soon stopped because he may have realised that the stone had a fault running through it which made it vulnerable. The rectangle was completed by another man and more crudely. In addition, two crosses have been carved in it at different times. Were they carved as a way of making the stone a Christian symbol? The two rings at either end may have been inserted to help carry the Stone when it was moved from its normal resting place in Scone Abbey into the open air for the inauguration ceremonies. The rings nestle in recesses cut into the surface of the Stone, allowing them to be flush with the surface. Each ring is attached to the Stone by means of a link which in turn is attached to a staple held in place by a lead-filled socket at each end of the stone.

'The staples have been filed down'

The staples have been filed down to make them protrude less from the side of the Stone. It is thought this must have been done when the Stone was being fitted into the Chair which Edward I had ordered to be made. It seems the Chair was made to the exact measurements of the Stone, and no-one had made allowances for the extra length caused by the staples sticking out. The thinned staples would have made them much weaker, but with the Stone encased in the Chair, and never expected to leave it, this would not have mattered.

Setting aside the mythical origins of the Stone, more prosaically, the Stone may have started out in life merely as a building block. One 19th-century expert suggested this could have been significant in itself, as unused masonry acquired powerful Judaeo–Christian symbolism from the psalmist's words *('The stone which the builders refused is become the head stone of the corner' Psalm 118:22)* quoted by Christ in three of the Gospels.The top of the Stone shows signs of having been worn smooth after the grooves had been cut. This suggests that the Stone may have been subject to wear by being walked or knelt on, or it might once have been used as a step. The sides of the Stone have been fairly precisely dressed, and this might have been done to allow the Stone to fit neatly into a hole in the floor as a capping stone, perhaps a manhole cover, allowing access into a royal tomb or a crypt where royal or saintly relics were kept. Was this how the Stone assumed its royal significance?

Its use as a capping stone would certainly explain the rings at either end, which could be used to lift the stone out of its recess. However, it is rather too small to support this theory, and if it had been a manhole cover the rings would probably have been inserted in the top of the Stone rather than in the sides.

Periodically throughout history efforts have been made to try to determine what the Stone actually consists of and, therefore, where it was quarried. In 1682 Henry Keepe, in one of the earliest books on Westminster Abbey, described it as being a bluish, steel-like colour with a pebble in it. In 1760 it was identified as a type of stone found generally around Scone, and 19th-century analysis confirmed this as the likely provenance of the Stone itself. When it was returned to Scotland in 1996, further examination by more sophisticated methods than were previously available concluded that it most probably came from old workings at Quarrymill, less than a mile south-east of Scone. Its hypothetical provenance in Egypt, Spain and Ireland was finally shown to be just a myth.

The Chair is commissioned

Once the Stone had arrived in London in 1296, Edward I ordered Adam, his goldsmith, to make an elaborate and expensive 'trophy case' in the shape of a bronze chair to house it. Details of the costs of the preliminary work are known from Adam's account. He first made a wooden chair, costing £5, to act as a template for casting the mouldings. He paid £12 5s. for 1,500 lbs of copper and tin to make the bronze, £10 for the wages of the men who cast it and a further £9 7s. 11d. to the men who worked on it in June and July 1297 after it was cast. Then suddenly, on 1 August, the bronze chair, along with several other projects, was abandoned as Edward saved money for his campaign in Flanders. He may well have grown tired of the idea of making an expensive chair for the Stone which was merely a relic of a territory he had conquered. Instead, he ordered a much less expensive wooden chair to be made by Walter of Durham – the Chair we have today. Master Walter had begun his career at Westminster in the mid-1260s. In 1297, when the Chair was commissioned, he was painting the royal apartments at Westminster: it was his last known work. We also know from Adam the goldsmith's original account that he made two leopards, painted and gilt, for the arms of Walter's Chair and for which he charged 13s 4d. Another account for 1300–1 shows that Walter of Durham was paid for making and painting a step at the foot of the Chair and a case to cover it – perhaps a canopy over it.

But what was behind Edward I's decision to encase the Stone in a chair? Did he envisage it as a 'Coronation Chair' in which the future kings of England would sit to be crowned? There is no evidence for this. Indeed, a 14th-century inventory in the Abbey muniments notes that the Stone was sent to the Abbey to be placed by St Edward's Shrine, but the phrase '… in order that the kings of England and Scotland might sit on it on the day of their coronation' has been crossed out. The Chair was installed on a small platform or step next to the altar in St Edward's Chapel, where it may have been used occasionally by the priest officiating at Mass or by the king when he entered the chapel during his Coronation to divest himself of his regalia.

The first firm evidence we have of the Chair being used at a Coronation ceremony is for the Coronation of Henry IV in 1399. But there is some circumstantial evidence it was used at earlier Coronations. There is a

OPPOSITE: *Edward VII (1902) was one of at least 28 monarchs to have been crowned in the Chair.*

contemporary illustration of Edward II sitting in what looks very like the Coronation Chair, which suggests he may have been crowned in it in 1307 – perhaps to honour his father's memory. His son, Edward III, may also have been crowned in it in 1327, but in 1328 he planned to send the Stone back to Scotland and one might ask, would he have done so if the Chair and Stone had played an important part in his Coronation? The Abbey's great painting of Richard II, the earliest contemporary portrait of an English monarch, shows the king sitting in the Chair, invested with his Coronation regalia, suggesting that he was crowned in it in 1377. But neither the Chair nor the Stone is mentioned or depicted in the *Liber Regalis*, thought to be the original order of ceremony for the Coronation of Richard II's wife, Anne of Bohemia, in 1381. And they are not mentioned in the 14th-century Litlyington Missal (compiled 1383/4) which sets out the order of Coronation as it then existed.

ABOVE: *Richard II in the artist's version of the Coronation Chair.*

OPPOSITE: *Edward II in what is probably the Coronation Chair.*

The first accurate depiction of the Chair appeared in Francis Sandford's magnificently illustrated history of the Coronation of James II (1685) published in 1687. The Chair is shown looking very much as it does today, though the four lions round the base are an earlier set which may have been added for the Coronation of Henry VIII in 1509.

By 1727 the Chair was showing signs of neglect and the first carved initials appeared on it. For George II's Coronation in that year the Chair clearly needed some attention. Four new lions were substituted – the ones we see today – and the Chair was strengthened with reinforcing rods in the base.

In 1767 John Carter made a careful measured drawing of the Chair. It shows that four-and-a-half of the original ten shields were still present around the grille where the Stone was kept (two on the left-hand side and two-and-a-half at the back) and the quatrefoil grille in the front of the Stone had disappeared.

Idealised 1807 drawing of the Chair, based on John Carter's 1767 drawing, showing shields round the base.

For the Coronation of George IV in 1821 the Chair was once more tidied up. This time two iron braces were placed under the Chair to take the weight of the Stone. The lions and the base were regilded and the pinnacles at the back were sawn off and new ones added. The following year, perhaps because the weight of history pricked the conscience of the keepers of the Chair, the new pinnacles were removed and the original ones nailed back on. But any care they might have lavished on the Chair clearly was insufficient to prevent the last remaining shields on the grille being lost – perhaps to souvenir hunters.

Then, with the passing of the decades, the Chair deteriorated further. Vergers would charge a small fee to allow people to sit in it, and more carved names appeared – again the handiwork of Westminster School boys. On the seat of the Chair one boy wrote: 'P Abbott slept here 5-6 July 1800'. And on the interior of the back of the Chair four cousins carved their names: Messrs N Curzon, T Lister, T Pelham and R Assheton.

At the Coronation of Queen Victoria in 1838, again finials were added to the gable and pinnacles but these were removed after the ceremony. It was during the preparations for Queen Victoria's Golden Jubilee celebration service in 1887 in the Abbey that the Chair suffered perhaps its most grievous injuries. The Office of Works removed the Chair from the Abbey, 'toned down' much of the Chair by painting it with a dark brown varnish and covered over the few remaining glazed lustres and white lead pastes with a browny-black paint. The 'improvements' caused concern in the House of Commons, and the Commissioner

of Works responsible was challenged about what had been done. At first he denied that there had been any change but later admitted that the Chair had been 'slightly darkened', though he said what had been done could easily be undone. Unfortunately, the process of undoing what he had done led to further damage. Some of the dark paint still clings to the woodwork and the paint was only partly scraped from the gilded gesso.

In preparing the Chair for Coronations over the centuries, further damage was done when cloth was nailed onto it – more than 18 yards of silver cloth for the Coronation of Queen Elizabeth I. Many of the nails which held the cloth are still there. One possible reason so many nails were used was to try to protect the cloth from souvenir hunters. Often, as soon as the procession had left the Abbey, there was a free-for-all as members of the congregation ripped pieces of cloth away. It may have been souvenir hunters who were also responsible for prising out what little glass decoration was left.

The Chair, damaged by the suffragette bomb in 1914, has lost a pinnacle.

The Coronation Chair attracted the attention of a political demonstration in 1914 when suffragettes hung a bag containing a small bomb on the right-hand pinnacle. The bomb consisted of two bicycle bells surrounded with nuts and bolts. It exploded, ripping the pinnacle from the Chair, blackening some of the woodwork and causing deep gashes on the Chair and on the wall behind it.

During the last century, whenever the Abbey was closed to prepare it for

a Coronation, the opportunity was taken to examine the Chair closely. In 1953 Stephen Rees Jones, the Head of Conservation and Technology at the Courtauld Institute in London, concluded that the decoration of the Chair probably took place in two distinct phases. The first one consisted of a simple scheme: an overall coating of lead-white paint with coloured motifs and vermilion lettering on the posts and pinnacles. The second was a later, more complex decorative scheme which included extensive gilding and the use of coloured glass and painted enamels covered with clear glass. When first made it must have been a spectacular sight. The gilded decorations included trellises of oak and vine leaves with birds, a grotesque, a knight on horseback and a green man, some of which is still visible. On the interior of the back was a depiction of a seated figure, probably King Edward the Confessor. By the time the Chair came to be reproduced in drawings and engravings, centuries later, only the lower part of the king's robe was left, with his slippered feet resting on a lion.

The exterior of the back, too, was heavily decorated with what were probably eight standing kings. It has been suggested that this second scheme was completed by about 1330 and was perhaps a celebratory act by the Abbot and Convent of Westminster to mark the fact that they had seen off Edward III's attempts to send the Stone back to Scotland and that it was now in their hands for good. But recently the theory that there were two decorative schemes has taken a knock. An inspection by the Hamilton Kerr Institute in 2004 concluded there were not, in fact, two separate decorative schemes but one single scheme. Marie Louise Sauerberg, who directed the conservation work on the Chair for the Institute, could find no evidence of two schemes. 'What Stephen Rees Jones noticed is in fact just a priming layer for the main decoration, with markings and annotations for what was to go on top. It's not substantial enough to amount to a complete scheme.' If that is the case, it raises the question: what did the Chair look like between about 1300, when it was made and about 1330 when it was decorated? Was it simply left as bare wood? There is obviously a mystery there,' says Marie Louise Sauerberg.

One possible way of finding out more about the exact age of the Chair would be to examine the tree rings in the wood to see when the wood was felled. To do that would require access to wood showing the end grain, and that might not be possible without taking the Chair off the base, something that might be very difficult to do. The bottom part of the Chair, with its four lions, was added in 1727, perhaps because the original base had rotted and been cut off. The Chair may then have been inserted into a groove which runs round the top of the new base. The Chair is fixed into the groove by four metal dowels, one at each corner, which extend down from each of the legs, through the four lions to protrude beneath their stomachs. The dowels are visible beneath the lions at each corner.

Before the next Coronation, when the Stone will be returned to the Chair,

Monarchs not crowned in the Coronation Chair

Edward V was deposed before the date fixed for his Coronation (6 July 1483).
Lady Jane Grey was proclaimed Queen on 10 July 1553 but her support collapsed nine days later.
Mary I, though she sat in the Coronation Chair for the homage, used a different chair for the crowning (1 October 1553).
Mary II became joint sovereign with her husband, William III so a second, duplicate, chair was made for their Coronation (11 April 1689).
Edward VIII abdicated before the date fixed for his Coronation (12 May 1937).

a survey will need to be carried out to make sure the Chair has not deteriorated to an extent that replacing the Stone might pose a risk. When in place, the Stone rests on two metal bars, each of which is screwed into wooden battens. It is not known how long these screws are, and therefore how secure the bars are. An x-ray would reveal this.

The 2004 inspection revealed further 'damage', this time resulting from good intentions. In the 1950s conservation waxes were fashionable and there are traces of these. And there are also traces of ordinary furniture polish which was used in ignorance in previous decades. Despite the damage, there are still hints of the Chair's original glory in the large areas of gilding which have survived – even though it is worn and dirty.

OPPOSITE TOP: *Gilded bird on the left arm of the chair.* BOTTOM: *Graffiti carved on the Chair.*

Scotland wants the Stone back

EDWARD I'S VICTORY OVER THE SCOTS in 1296 did not signal the end of hostilities between the two countries. In 1314 Robert Bruce gained a decisive victory over Edward II's forces at Bannockburn and during the following decade he made a series of raids into northern England. In 1324 he tried to negotiate a peace treaty under which Edward II would renounce claims to Scotland, and at the same time demanded the return of the Stone of Destiny. Edward II was having none of it. He said that in the context of all the other demands the Stone was insignificant and, in any case, it was his father who had taken it and its surrender would negate his father's victory. It was stalemate. Four years later, the young Edward III agreed to Scottish independence under the Treaty of Edinburgh-Northampton. Though the Treaty itself did not specify that the Stone should be returned, the 15-year-old King issued a writ in which he ordered the Abbot of Westminster and the monks to hand it over to the Sheriffs of London, who would make sure it got into the hands of his Mother, Queen Isabella, the real power behind the throne. She was in the north and intended to use it as a bargaining counter to get compensation for the English disinherited of their wealth in Scotland. But the King and his mother were to be frustrated in their endeavours. The Abbot and the people of Westminster refused to release the Stone, perhaps because they regarded it as a tangible sign of victory and were not at all happy that the King had given in so easily to Scottish demands. Thirty years later there was more talk of the Stone's return, but nothing came of it.

When James VI of Scotland became James I of England in 1603, and was crowned at Westminster Abbey, one of the ancient myths about the Stone seemed to come true – that wherever the Stone was, there a Scot would rule. About its ownership there could be no further argument: in effect, James had recovered what Edward I had stolen. More than 250 years would pass before, once again, the Stone caused political hackles to rise. In 1884, during a period of Irish unrest, the MP for Barnsley, C S Kenney, complained that the notice on the Coronation Chair in the Abbey had been changed to exclude any reference to the Stone being the original Stone on which Irish kings were inaugurated – even though we know now that the Stone had never been in Ireland. It was the turn of members of a Fenian organisation to try

'...there a Scot would rule'

to seize it. A plot was laid and supporters came over from America to help. Their plan was to hide in the Abbey and, at night, to seize the Stone and pass it out through a window. But someone tipped off the police, who mounted guard, and the opportunity never came.

For many years the Chair stood at the west end of Edward the Confessor's Shrine.
OVERLEAF: *The Chair now stands in the ambulatory.*

The rise of the Scottish Nationalist movement in the early 1920s once more revived the controversy over the Stone. A Private Member's Bill was introduced into the House of Commons in 1924 calling for the Stone to be returned to Scotland. It passed its first reading by 201 votes to 171, but the Government refused to support it and it fell. It did however raise the Stone's profile. Five years later a Glasgow monumental mason, who was to play an important part in the successful 1950s theft of the Stone, made a replica of it, which he planned to substitute for the original, but nothing came of that plan because, once again, the authorities were tipped off.

In 1930, on orders from Ramsay MacDonald's government, the Public Record Office in London restored to its Edinburgh counterpart many official documents which had been taken from Scotland by Edward I. One demonstrator paraded along the Royal Mile in Edinburgh with a placard proclaiming 'England disgorges some of the loot, but where is the Stone of Destiny?' Just 20 years later the Stone would indeed be back in Scotland – not handed over officially, but spirited there in an audacious and headline-grabbing stunt which reverberated around the world.

Scotland helps itself

WHEN THE STONE OF DESTINY WAS officially returned to Scotland in 1996 by Prime Minister, John Major, it was not the first time it had been over the Scottish border since it was captured by Edward I. In 1950 it was stolen by young Scottish Nationalists who took it to Scotland where it resided for three months before being returned. The theft was breathtaking in its execution, not because of the planning which went into it – there was precious little – but for the quite extraordinary luck which enabled the group to succeed. They became heroes and, to many in Scotland, they still are.

The man behind the theft, Ian Hamilton, was 25 and passionate about Scottish independence. As a small boy in the 1930s he remembered seeing a picture of the lone demonstrator in the Royal Mile with her sandwich board asking '...where is the Stone of Destiny?' His mother had told him the story of the Stone and it was an image which stuck. The sense of injustice it provoked never left him and led him to a simple solution: if the English wouldn't hand the Stone back, he would take it back.

His first mistake was to go to Glasgow's Mitchell Library and, under his own name, take out every book he could find on the Abbey and the Stone of Destiny. Those library slips were to become the only pieces of firm evidence the police had incriminating him. He went to London on a reconnaissance mission and discovered that, after the Abbey closed, it seemed to be empty, with no army of cleaners moving in. He hung around the Abbey all night to see what sort of police presence there was and found there was very little.

'... it was an image which stuck'

To carry out his plan he needed accomplices. He recruited a young domestic science teacher, Kay Mathieson, as the driver, and a 24-year-old engineering student, Gavin Vernon, who hired an old car – a Ford Anglia. At the last minute a fourth man, Alan Stuart, joined the team with a second, more reliable, car of the same make. These four were young unknowns, but also in on the plan were the group's better-known backers: John MacCormick, the founder of the Home Rule movement and Lord Rector of Glasgow University, and Bertie Gray, a monumental sculptor and member of Glasgow's Town Council. Gray owned a mason's yard and when Hamilton wanted to find out the weight of the Stone, Gray showed him the copy of the Stone he had made 20 years earlier for a plot to substitute it for the real one, a plot which was betrayed to the

The thieves: Ian Hamilton (centre) with Gavin Vernon (left) and Alan Stuart.

police before it got off the ground. On the evening of 22 December 1950, the four young unknowns set off for London.

It was a difficult journey through snow and ice but they finally arrived the following afternoon. They decided to go for the Stone that evening. With a large jemmy in a sling under his arm, Hamilton entered the Abbey during visiting hours and hid under a cleaner's trolley in the north transept. His plan was to wait until the early hours, let the others in by the Poets' Corner door opposite the Houses of Parliament, and take the Stone out the same way. Shortly after the Abbey closed at 6.00pm he decided to move to St Paul's Chapel nearby for better cover. As he was creeping there in his stockinged feet he heard the night-watchman's jangling keys and a torch was shone in his face. Hamilton bluffed it out, saying that he had been locked in by mistake, and gave a false name and address. The night-watchman believed him and even asked him if he had enough money to find a place for the night before showing him out. Hamilton said later he never forgot the night-watchman's kindness.

With the first attempt a failure, Hamilton and his co-conspirators planned a second attempt for the following night – Christmas Eve. This time they would jemmy their way into the Abbey after it was closed for the day. That evening the three men approached the Abbey's Poets' Corner door only to

ABOVE: *The Stone was dragged through a door beside the high altar and down the steps to Poets' Corner.*
OPPOSITE: *The Confessor's Chapel, with the tomb of Edward I in the foreground*

find their way barred by a padlocked gate. They managed to bypass this by breaking into a row of sheds beside the gate which gave them access right up to the door itself. Having got so far, and satisfied themselves that it could be done, they retreated and went to collect the fourth member of the team, Kay Mathieson, who was spending the night in a hotel near St Pancras because she was unwell. Then came another problem which could have jeopardised their whole plan. When they arrived at the hotel, in the early hours of the morning to wake her up, the owner of the hotel became suspicious and phoned the police. The police questioned them but, once more, they bluffed their way through.

Leaving one car in a car park near the Abbey, all four of them approached the Abbey in the second car and backed it up a small lane by the Poets' Corner door. With a fearsome-sounding crack they jemmied open the door and found themselves, at last, inside the Abbey. Quickly they made their way to Edward the Confessor's Chapel and jemmied off the bar in front of the Stone cavity. They pushed the Stone out and put it on Hamilton's coat lying on the floor. As Hamilton pulled at one of the Stone's rings, to his astonishment it came away – together with a quarter of the Stone. The fault line in the Stone, which had been noticed 700 years before, had at last given way and the Stone was in two pieces. Hamilton picked up the smaller bit, staggered with it out of Poets'

'It was too late to get a bed for the night'

Corner door and put it into the back seat of the car. He went back into the Abbey and swung the other, bigger piece down the altar steps and dragged it to the Poets' Corner door. They had the Stone, now they had to get it away from the Abbey.

At this point they faced another potential crisis. As Hamilton got to the door he saw Kay Mathieson start to drive the car down the lane towards the road. As he dashed forward to tell her to get the car back under cover he saw a policeman coming across the road towards them. Hamilton got into the car and he and Kay went into a clinch like a courting couple. The policeman wanted to know what they were doing parked up by the Abbey at 5.00am on Christmas morning, to which they replied that they were down from Scotland to see the sights and had decided to sleep in the car as it was too late to get a bed for the night. Satisfied, instead of going on his way the policeman took off his helmet and lit a cigarette. At this point they heard grunting, then a thump, from the direction of the sheds. The other two were still struggling with the bigger piece of the Stone, not realising what was happening outside. The policeman joked that it sounded as if the night-watchman had fallen down the stairs. The two in the car said goodnight and drove off and the policeman went on his way. When they had got clear, Hamilton transferred the smaller bit of stone into the boot of the car and left Kay to drive away while he went back to get the second car to retrieve the other part of the Stone. But he couldn't find his car keys. Then it dawned on him: they were in the pocket of his coat which they had used to drag the Stone out of the Abbey. He re-entered the sheds beside the Abbey and discovered the bigger bit of Stone where Alan and Gavin had left it – but no Gavin or Alan. He went into the Abbey the third time that evening to look for his coat, but in vain. He returned to the car park, expecting Gavin and Alan to be there. There was no sign of them – but there was the car. He decided that if his friends had his coat they would have found his car keys and driven back to the Abbey. He guessed the keys must have fallen out of his coat pocket in the Abbey as it was being dragged along. A fourth time that night he returned to the Abbey and on his hands and knees retraced his steps, trying to find the keys. Just as he was giving up he accidentally trod on them by the door. He left the Abbey, got his car, backed it up as close to the door as he could and with a huge effort managed to drag the Stone to it and heave it into the back seat. At this same moment, at the other end of the Abbey, the night-watchman was telephoning the police to report that the Stone had gone.

Hamilton now drove over Westminster Bridge and found himself on unfamiliar roads. As he drove around, hopelessly lost, he suddenly saw Alan and Gavin ahead of him. They had left the Abbey with the coat to get the car but could not find the keys in the pocket of the coat, which they then left in the car park.

The three men drove south, hid the Stone in some brambles and drove back to the car park to retrieve the coat before speeding out of London. By this time, word of the theft had been broadcast and when Hamilton telephoned one of his backers in Glasgow he was told that the whole of Scotland was mad with excitement. What had started as a dream, was now a reality – and the hunt was on for the culprits. Roadblocks had been set up on the roads to Scotland and the police were out in force. It was clearly too dangerous for them to try to take the Stone back to Scotland now, so they collected the Stone from the brambles and drove south, towards Kent, where they hid it in a shallow grave. Then came the long journey back to Scotland. Two weeks later they retrieved the smaller piece of Stone from Kay Mathieson, who had been staying in Birmingham with a friend. The one clue which they had inadvertently left behind was Hamilton's watch, which had come off in the Abbey when they were manhandling the heavy Stone.

The disappearance of the Stone was the main item of news that Christmas and word quickly spread around the world. The Dean of Westminster, Alan Don, was himself a Scot and was therefore doubly embarrassed by the theft.

The Stone is found in Arbroath Abbey.

He broadcast an emotional appeal on the radio, saying he would go to the ends of the earth to get the Stone back, describing the theft as a 'cunningly planned and carefully executed crime'. He had no knowledge of just how badly planned and carelessly executed the crime had been. In Scotland, more and more people were becoming aware of who had carried out the theft – but such was their loyalty to the cause that none gave the game away.

Hamilton's mission was not yet over. The Stone may have been taken, but it was still in England, hidden in undergrowth. Two weeks after the theft they borrowed a car and once more set out south across the border. It took them 24 hours to drive to Kent and to the Stone's burial place just outside Rochester. When they got there they found, to their dismay, that an encampment of gypsies had set up next to where the Stone lay. Once they understood the situation, the gypsies helped load the Stone into the car, where it substituted for the passenger seat and, with Hamilton sitting on it, they drove back to Scotland. Once over the border they poured a libation of whisky over it to toast their success. They themselves were the

The Stone as icon

1868: The Dean of Westminster, Arthur Stanley, said the Stone was 'the one primeval monument which binds the whole empire together.'

1921: Freemasons claimed it was the top of the altar on which Abraham prepared to sacrifice his son.

1924: The Royal Commission on Historical Monuments called it 'That strange palladium of the Empire.'

1937: Author Adam Rutherford called it 'The most precious emblem of the greatest empire the world has ever known.'

toast of Scotland and even the police efforts to find them were half-hearted. 'Sure we're looking for them,' one policeman was quoted as saying, 'but not so damned hard as we'll find them!'

The Stone was professionally mended and taken to a friend's factory at Bonnybridge where it lay hidden. Eventually, Hamilton was persuaded that, the deed done and the point made, they must give it up. They placed it on the altar in Arbroath Abbey, chosen because it was where the Arbroath Declaration had been signed in 1320 by the Lords, Commons and Clergy of Scotland, reaffirming their right to live their lives in their own way. The police swooped, collected the Stone and, to a roar of disapproval in Scotland, took it south again. Hamilton never saw the Stone again.

The Stone returns to London

THE DISCOVERY OF THE STONE OF DESTINY in Arbroath Abbey came as a huge relief to Westminster Abbey and especially to Dean Don. It had been missing for more than three months. But it would be nearly a year before it was put back into the Coronation Chair, because the Government, having recovered the Stone, was now tempted to hand it back to Scotland officially. It was only the death of King George VI in 1952 – and persistent lobbying by Dean Don – which finally led to its being restored to the Chair and once more put on display.

Within a month or two of the theft it became obvious who had stolen it. The four students were arrested. Hamilton's three colleagues made full confessions but they did not reveal where they had hidden it. A decision then had to be taken on whether they should be prosecuted. It was a politically sensitive issue because, as the Attorney General, Sir Hartley Shawcross, reported to the Cabinet, opinion in Scotland was very much divided. Though the general view was that the Stone should be returned to the Abbey, there was an equally general view that if those responsible were prosecuted there would be widespread, strong and very hostile reaction in Scotland. Shawcross was still undecided but felt that any prosecution would not bring the Stone back and might well result in its permanent disappearance.

It was a few days after the Cabinet meeting, on 12 April, and no doubt as a result of some discreet arm-twisting, that the Stone mysteriously reappeared in Arbroath Abbey. It was delivered back to Westminster and put in the vault beneath the Abbey's Islip Chapel, where it had been hidden during the war.

With the Stone now safe, one of the arguments against prosecuting the culprits – that the Stone might disappear permanently – had been removed. But there remained a number of reasons, both legal and political, why a prosecution would be difficult. Less than a week after the Stone had been recovered, Shawcross finally decided not to prosecute. He felt that it would be difficult to prove that the students' intention had been permanently to deprive the owner of the Stone – legally an essential ingredient in the definition of theft – and he also did not want to give the students what they would regard as 'the triumph of acquittal or the martyrdom of a conviction'.

'It was put in the vault'

But if they were not to be prosecuted for theft, could they not be prosecuted for damaging the Coronation Chair? In removing the Stone they had

caused a slight split in the oak seat, and the wooden batten which had held the Stone in position had been broken. Shawcross's view was that any prosecution which did not involve the Stone itself would be an anti-climax. And, in any case, by this time he felt that the public had got bored with the subject and that there was no public pressure for a prosecution.

The Government now had to decide what to do with the Stone: whether it should be restored to the Chair or whether it should, after all, be returned to Scotland.

Legally, the Stone did not belong to the Government – but neither did it belong to Westminster Abbey. A Cabinet briefing paper on the ownership of the Stone made it clear that it was the property of the Sovereign, who could dispose of it as he thought fit 'unfettered by the charter or statutes of Westminster Abbey'. After Edward I had become its owner by right of capture in 1296 there was no evidence that the King or his successors had ever relinquished that ownership. The Stone had been *lodged* with the Abbey and it was in the Abbey's custody, but it was never *given* to the Abbey, nor was it dedicated to the service of religion.

The Secretary of State for Scotland was against returning the Stone to Scotland as it would tend 'either to be looked upon as a dead symbol of an extinct Scottish monarchy, like the Scottish Regalia now on display at Edinburgh Castle, or as a symbol of Scottish aspirations'. He also made it clear that if it were returned to Scotland it should be placed in St Margaret's Chapel in the Castle. Another idea discussed at the time was for the Stone to go on a tour of Commonwealth countries 'as a symbol of the common crown'.

In May 1951 the Cabinet considered the various options, but decided to postpone any decision for a year because they felt that any sudden decision to return the Stone to Scotland would be seen as a concession to the recent act of vandalism. At this point there was a debate in the House of Lords, at which every speaker bar one urged that the Stone should go back to Scotland. This worried Dean Don. He told the Government that he could not receive instructions about what to do with the Stone from anyone but the King himself as Visitor of the Abbey and, speaking as a Scot, he said he felt it would be deplorable if it was removed from Westminster where it symbolised the union of England and Scotland under the Crown. At that time he accepted the general opinion that nothing should be done for a year to avoid stirring things up, but a few months later, in August, the Dean seemed to have changed his mind about waiting. Perhaps he feared that opinion was crystallising in favour of returning the Stone to Scotland. He contacted the Prime Minister's office again, saying he felt the Stone should be returned to the Chair soon, because any delay in exhibiting it might be taken as a sign of weakness. He suggested it could be replaced in a simple ceremony at which he, as a Scot, would be present, along with a representative of the Church of Scotland. That,

OPPOSITE: *Back in the Abbey for the Queen's Coronation. The Chair faces the altar for the service, here it has been turned round for public display.*

Is the Stone genuine?

Throughout its history there have been claims that the Stone of Scone, now in Edinburgh Castle, is not the genuine article. Was Edward I deceived into taking the wrong Stone? If the monks at Scone Abbey knew that he was coming, did they perhaps hew out a duplicate and hide the real one? It is possible, but unlikely, that Edward I would have been so easily deceived, as two of his associates would probably have seen the genuine article when they attended the inauguration of John Balliol in 1292. Again, the Scots complained of the loss of their stone in 1306, but they would hardly have done so if Edward had taken the wrong one.

There have also been claims that, after it was stolen from the Abbey in 1950, the Scots returned a replica. But the man who took the Stone then, Ian Hamilton, dismisses such a claim, and the Dean and Chapter at the Abbey were certain that the genuine Stone was returned.

Having said this, there are puzzling aspects to some of the original medieval descriptions of the Stone as a throne or seat or chair, because the Stone, as we know it, is not large enough to act as a seat. One recent commentator remarked that 11 inches (the height of the Stone) was the height of a decent-sized Victorian chamber pot and any king sitting on it would have looked utterly ridiculous with his knees about his ears. One description has the chair 'carved by a careful craftsman', another that it was a 'jewel' and another that it was 'large' or 'great'. The likely explanation is that the Stone itself was encased *within* a chair or throne. In any case, the chroniclers who thus described the seat may not have actually seen it. And there is another puzzle. The ancient seals depicting Scottish kings on their thrones give no inkling that they are sitting on the Stone, though it is possible that the Stone is encased within the throne and concealed from view.

The conclusion must be that the Stone is the very one which has acted as the talisman giving authority to the kings and queens of first Scotland, and then the United Kingdom, for more than 1000 years.

he hoped, would signify the burying of the hatchet. His lobbying had little effect. By September, the Government had another excuse to delay the decision: the King was now too ill to be approached about the Stone. In addition, a General Election was due, so any final decision would have to wait until the new Government had taken office. By December, with a new Prime Minister, Winston Churchill, in office, Alan Don was becoming impatient and wrote again to the Lord Chancellor, urging action. Still nothing happened. Then, on 6 February 1952, King George VI died. Now the matter suddenly became very urgent. Just two days after the King's death, the Lord Chancellor and the Secretary of State for Scotland both argued that the Stone should be replaced in the Chair without delay. The decision to restore it to the Chair was taken on 20 February and the Stone was replaced with no ceremony. Churchill made a brief statement in Parliament and the Chair was once more put on display, with new security devices to protect it. Publicity was minimal and the decision caused hardly a ripple.

The Queen – crowned in the Coronation Chair.

As the owner of the Stone, the Queen's thoughts on whether the Stone should be returned to Scotland were presumably important. An intriguing clue as to what they were is given in a letter from Jock Colville, Winston Churchill's Private Secretary. On 1 April 1952 he wrote to the Dowager Countess of Airlie, 'I think a strong argument against returning the Stone to St Giles is that the late King felt so strongly on the subject… I am sure it would upset the Queen very much if she were asked to do this, especially as she knows what her father felt on the subject.' It was 46 years later that the Queen finally approved the decision to send the Stone back to Scotland.

The Stone leaves the Abbey – officially

THE FERVOUR GENERATED BY THE 1950 theft of the Stone, and the excitement with which its return to Scotland was greeted, made a lasting impact. The idealism and naivety of youth had delighted all of Scotland and the country rejoiced in what appeared to them as the English establishment's discomfiture. The next time the Stone of Destiny was to cross the Scottish border the frisson of victory was distinctly absent. In 1996 it was sent back to Scotland officially by order of the Prime Minister, John Major, and with the approval of the Queen. But instead of approbation, many greeted the gesture with a bemused contempt. There had been no groundswell of public opinion demanding the Stone back to which the Prime Minister was responding. The decision came out of the blue, and the Prime Minister was pilloried in the media for what some saw as a political stunt. But from the Government point of view the decision was taken after a great deal of thought and because of the particular circumstances which prevailed at the time.

The first that the Abbey authorities knew of the decision to return the Stone to Scotland was only shortly before the decision was made public. The Dean of Westminster, Michael Mayne, was visited by the Prime Minister's Ecclesiastical Secretary, John Holroyd, who told him that in two days' time the Prime Minister, with the Queen's approval, was to announce that the Stone of Scone was to be sent to Scotland where it would be placed in a museum. The Dean was astonished – a reaction which quickly gave way to anger. 'I felt we were being presented with a *fait accompli* about something which was of huge significance, not just to the Abbey but to the nation,' he said later, 'yet we had been given just 48 hours' notice.' The Dean was told that the Abbey had not been informed earlier for fear they might leak the news – an argument the Dean found 'grossly discourteous'. The Dean called an emergency meeting of his colleagues at which they decided to get legal advice on whether the Government had the right to take such a decision. The Abbey's lawyers quickly established that the Stone belonged to the Queen and that, as she had agreed to the decision, there was little the Dean and Chapter could do. However, they felt that even if they could not reverse the decision, at least they could influence the way it was carried out.

'They might leak the news'

Detail from Ninian Comper's Edward I window in the nave showing the stone as Jacob's pillow.

The Dean asked for a meeting with the Prime Minister. 'I don't know that we were hopeful of the eventual outcome but I wanted to put certain points to the Prime Minister which might not have been considered and which might affect the statement which was to be made to Parliament.' It was an uncomfortable meeting. 'I put it to him that the Stone and Chair were of a single integrity – the reliquary with the relic in it – which was used at the most sacred moment of Coronation. I asked him, by separating the Stone from the Chair, literally wrenching them apart, and putting the Stone not in a Church but in a museum, what had that to say about how one viewed the monarchy?' It was clear from Major's reaction that he had not thought about this. I don't think the Prime Minister had much sense of history or of the spiritual or sacramental nature of things. John Major got quite angry with me at one point which, I was told, was a good sign as it showed he had been listening. But I did not feel very hopeful.' The meeting had little effect and the announcement was made.

The decision was welcomed by both Tony Blair, the Leader of the Labour opposition, who was later to become Prime Minister, and by a spokesman for the Liberal Democrats, the other main opposition party. But it caused an outcry in the Press and many column inches were filled with details about the history of the Stone and especially the 1950 theft. If the Prime Minister had expected rejoicing in Scotland he was to be disappointed. Scottish Labour MPs reacted with derision. They wanted devolution, constitutional reform and jobs. All they got was the Stone. Academics, too, were aghast. In *The Times* two eminent Cambridge University medieval art historians said that divorcing the Stone from the Chair marked 'a real cultural loss and diminution of our nation's sense of the past'. Another commentator, Nick Aitchson, wrote, 'Scots wanted a better future, not a symbol of the past', and the London *Evening Standard* described it as 'an act of indefensible vandalism'. The right-wing *Spectator* magazine deplored the way John Major had implicated the monarch in party politics. The fact was that the Conservative Party had few friends in Scotland and Major's decision was seen as a sop to the Scots to curry favour.

The Secretary of State for Scotland, however, rejected this interpretation of events. He explained that the Government papers relating to the 1950 theft of the Stone were due for release shortly and they showed that, in 1950, the Government was sympathetic to Scotland's claims to ownership. Once this became known the clamour for the Stone to be returned would start all over again. Partly to avoid it becoming an election issue the Government decided to bite the bullet. The politicians involved realised, too late, that they had caused unnecessary insult to the Abbey authorities and they regretted that.

Soon after the annuncement was made the Dean and Chapter issued a strongly worded statement saying, 'As the successors of those abbots of Westminster and Deans and Chapters who have been guardians of the Stone for so many centuries, we must continue to urge those who are advising the Queen in this matter to take full account of the symbolic and emotional significance of the Stone, its integral connection with the Coronation Chair… and its intimate association with the sacrament of Coronation.'

They did not want the Stone to be regarded merely as a museum piece and said that its religious associations should be considered most carefully and respected in any decisions about its future.

OPPOSITE: *The Stone is carried from the Abbey as the clergy remain 'boot-faced'.*

The Dean and Chapter wanted the Stone's removal from the Abbey to be as low-key as possible. Their magnanimity and generosity were appreciated by Historic Scotland, the Government Agency which had the unenviable task of descending on the Abbey and taking the Stone away. It was agreed that Historic Scotland's staff, in close collaboration with the Abbey's Clerk of Works, would do the job. A piece of sandstone of similar size was cut and used for rehearsals. On the evening of 14 November a team from Scotland

'Two slots had to be cut in the foam'

waited in a side street for the last visitors to leave the Abbey and then entered through the Poets' Corner door – the same door Ian Hamilton had jemmied open 50 years before.

When they inspected the Stone they found it to be a very tight fit, with no clearance for the iron rings past the Chair's arms. The painted gesso inside the arms of the chair would need protecting with thin sheets of plastic as it was vital there should be no lateral movement of the stone which might damage the Chair, but the plastic would further reduce the clearance. Historic Scotland were also concerned about the integrity of the 1951 cement repair which joined the two pieces of the Stone together.

The metal grille surrounding the Chair was removed and then the Chair seat. By 10.00pm the Chair had been surrounded by scaffolding and two plastic lifting straps had been passed under the Stone, parallel to the iron bars on the Chair itself. With infinite care the Stone was hoisted out.

The Stone was placed on the specially made hand-carrier – like a stretcher – and a lid lowered over it to secure it. Unfortunately, the lid would not pass over the projecting staples to which the links were attached because, in making the lid, the designer had forgotten to take into account the overall length of the Stone plus the iron staples which protruded at the side – exactly the same mistake the original maker of the Chair had made nearly 700 years before. Two slots had to be cut in the foam packing material lining the lid.

The lid was sealed with a wax seal and the precious package was carried from the Chapel, set on an electric trolley and wheeled to the lantern (the area in front of the high altar) where it remained for the rest of the night.

The next morning the team returned at 6.30am, to be met by the Dean and Chapter. The departure of the Stone was to be marked by a simple ceremony before Matins. The Dean and a representative of Historic Scotland signed copies of a receipt for the Stone and it was brought down to the west doors shortly after 7.00am. The west doors were opened and, to a dazzle of flashes from waiting photographers, the Stone was carried out, followed by the senior Abbey Clergy and the Receiver General. The Chapter had made a conscious decision to remain 'boot-faced' as they stood at the west door to see the Stone off. 'None of us would turn on any semblance of charm or approval. No-one broke ranks,' said Canon Colin Semper. Their demeanour did not go unnoticed. The *Guardian* newspaper commented, 'Their faces said it all.' The Stone was loaded into a police Land Rover which set off for Scotland with a police escort.

The police led the way through the early morning traffic as far as the start of the M1, after which the convoy travelled north in close formation. After spending the night in Gateshead, the convoy eventually arrived at Coldstream Bridge where Michael Forsyth, the Secretary of State for Scotland, who had long wanted the Stone returned to Scotland and who had persuaded John Major to make the decision, was waiting to escort it over.

Back home – for good

THE MORNING AFTER THE STONE ARRIVED IN Scotland it was taken to the National Museums of Scotland x-radiography laboratory in Edinburgh, where the 1951 repair was examined. X-rays revealed there were three metal rods within the Stone holding the repair together. The two main rods ran parallel to each other across the break, the third rod was almost right angles to them. The experts recognised that this type of repair was very difficult to achieve and were not surprised the detached lump was slightly misaligned. Historic Scotland did not want to have to repeat the repair, as they planned to put the Stone on display in time for St Andrew's Day in two weeks' time. They also felt that another attempt at a repair might cause further damage, besides which the 1951 repair was now part of the Stone's history. The x-rays showed that all of the rods were solid. There had been rumours in the 1950s that one rod had been hollow and that Bertie Gray, who had repaired it, had hidden a message in the Stone saying that one day it would return to Scotland – a suggestion that Ian Hamilton had denied. The Stone was carefully cleaned and recorded in meticulous detail for the first time.

The careful examination did reveal one surprise. Stephen Gordon, Historic Scotland's senior stone conservator, found a small circular spot of red sealing wax on the back of the Stone. It was sealing a hole, 4–5mms (·25ins) in diameter, drilled into the Stone, inside which was a lead tube. This contained two tightly rolled pieces of paper which formed a triangle measuring 33mms (1·5ins) x 90mms (3·5ins) x 95mms (3·8ins) and which had faded, largely indecipherable writing on both sides. Was this the mysterious message said to have been concealed in the Stone by Bertie Gray? The truth was even more surprising and was revealed in 2003 by the Society of Antiquaries of Scotland, when it published the proceedings of a conference on the Stone which had been held in 1997. It transpired that in 1973 the Surveyor of the Fabric at the Abbey had instructed the lead tube to be inserted as a security measure following a further unsuccessful attempt at a theft of the Stone during which the Stone had been dragged halfway out of the Chair, setting off alarms. The tube was inserted so that if the Stone were stolen again and recovered it could be identified as genuine by matching the triangle of paper with the larger piece from which it had been cut and which was kept at the Abbey.

After a lengthy consultation exercise it had been decided to put the Stone in

'There were three metal rods'

'It was taken first to St Giles'

Edinburgh Castle alongside the Honours of Scotland (the Scottish regalia) having regard to 'history, accessibility and security.' The decision was not universally welcomed. The academic, Nick Aitchison, wrote in his book on the Stone: 'The Stone has nothing to do with the Honours which date from the 16th century and reflect a very different style of kingship. And the Stone's only historical association with Edinburgh Castle was that it was kept there temporarily on its way south after it was seized by Edward I.'

When the day arrived for the Stone to be put on display, it was taken first to St Giles Cathedral for a special service, attended by the Duke of York, then to the castle. Thousands turned out to watch – but with little sense of triumph.

At a conference on the Stone the following year the journalist Neal Ascherson said that the response of the people of Scotland to having the Stone back was grudging, muted and curious rather than openly welcoming. 'It was good to have the Stone back, good but not transforming.' For the Scots what mattered about the Stone was its absence – taken away by an English king. The Scots had nurtured a grievance. 'The significance of the Stone as wrongfully acquired English/British property almost entirely eclipsed any ritual or symbolic importance it retained as lost Scottish property. The 1950 repossession had been perceived as an authentic Scottish act, which, if it had proved permanent, would have fully compensated for the loss of a grievance. The 1996 return of the Stone, on the other hand, felt like an act of calculated largesse from outwith Scotland, and therefore offered no such compensating shot in the national arm. An occasion for ingratitude was offered, and it was not missed.' The irony of the whole saga is that John Major's decision to return the Stone to Scotland had no impact on the Conservative Party's fortunes in Scotland (if that had been the intention) because at the 1997 General Election the Conservatives did not win a single Scottish seat. Later, in 1998, real political power was devolved to Scotland with the setting-up of the first Scottish Parliament since 1707.

Today, instead of resting in the ancient oak Chair made for it 700 years ago, the Stone of Destiny rests in a glass display case. It will briefly flicker into life at the next Coronation when it returns to the Abbey, but for most of the time it is merely a museum piece.

The return of the Stone to Scotland did have one beneficial spin-off for the Abbey. The Coronation Chair is a key attraction for the millions of tourists who flock to the Abbey and now, with the Stone gone, there was no perceived obligation to keep the Chair in St Edward's Chapel where it had been for 700 years and where there had always been something of a tourist logjam. The Abbey, therefore, had no qualms about bringing the Chair out of the Chapel, as part of its scheme to 'Recover the Calm', and installing it where tourists could admire it more easily, at the foot of King Henry V's tomb. There it will remain until it is placed in front of the Abbey's high altar for the next Coronation – once more complete with the Stone of Destiny.